RAMOLOGY

Note to Self

by

R.A. McAlpine

BOSS LADY PRESS | HOUSTON

Copyright © 2019 by R. A. McAlpine.

All rights reserved. No part of this publication may be reproduced, distributed or transmitted in any form or by any means, including photocopying, recording, or other electronic or mechanical methods, without the prior written permission of the publisher, except in the case of brief quotations embodied in critical reviews and certain other noncommercial uses permitted by copyright law. For permission requests, write to the publisher, addressed "Attention: Permissions Coordinator," at the address below.

Boss Lady Press
40 FM 1960 West, #141
Houston, TX 77090
281-826-9576
www.bossladypress.com

Costume design and Concepts by Reginald and Lisa T. McAlpine
BRIX Investments Group LLC
www.BrixInvestmentsGroup.com

Book Layout by Darshell McAlpine – www.bossladypress.com

Edited by Janelle Shields

Cover Design by Domonique Bowie – www.domoniquedesigns1906.com

Photos by Opia Photography – www.opiaphotography.zenfolio.com

Ramology: Note to Self/R. A. McAlpine—1st ed.
ISBN: 13: 978-1-7325113-3-0
Library of Congress Control Number: 2019901140

Table of Contents

ACKNOWLEDGEMENTS i
PREFACE iii
PARDON ME 2
SEX SELLS 4
THE HUSTLE 6
STILL HUNTING 8
RACISM 10
GREATNESS 12
RELIGIOUS 14
STILL RISING 16
100 MILES 18
I APOLOGIZE 20
FOREVER MORE 22
QUALITY 24
TAKE A KNEE 26
A FATHER'S LOVE 28
BASTARD CHILD 30
REVELATION NOT FOUND 32
STILL BLAZING 34
MA'AT CREED 36
BLACK CRIMINALIZATION 38
MY SON 40
BLACKBIRD 42
TORN 44
MEDITATE ON THIS 46
THE PURGE 48
MY SEED 50
RECKONING 52

ENIGMA	54
FORSAKEN	56
MY COUNTRY 'TIS OF THEE	58
INNER PEACE	60
LITTLE BLACK BOY	62
THE TRUTH	64
SPOKEN WORD	66
DAMNED IF I KNOW	68
ONE DAY AT A TIME	70
RETURN TO SENDER	72
LEGACY	74
ALWAYS	76
SHUT-'EM DOWN	78
ELEVATION	80
BLACK RIVER	82
THIS OLD HOUSE	84
FIGHT THE POWER	86
DOWN ASS	88
LILY	90
STAY WOKE	92
WRITER'S WRITE	94
LYNCHING	96
CAUSE AND EFFECT	98
HIP-HOP	100
NOTE TO SELF	102

Acknowledgements

Each step within our journey is accompanied by someone significant to our ultimate goal. These people inspire you and motivate your sense of self. They push you beyond yourself so that you can experience the greater you. I have had such an awesome support team by my side throughout the creation of *Ramology: Note to Self*. I have become the author that I am today in large part because of them.

To my eternal soulmate and wife, Lisa: you are the oxygen that fans my flames. Your love and support have walked alongside me from undergrad to grad, and now into this new chapter of our lives as authors. You have healed my heart and encouraged my soul to dream dreams again. Our love is the gift that keeps on giving.

To my mother: I have learned from you the gift of grit, perseverance and stick-to-itiveness. This has allowed me to push through even when those I love spoke ill of me or treated me cruelly. You have taught me that life might bruise your body, but you can prevent it from crushing your spirit.

To my young ones:

Reggie: God placed you in my path to teach me what real manhood looks like as I developed into a father. I thought I knew a lot until I realized how much I didn't know. You are my first "man" child and I am so proud of the man you've become.

Sajee: You have taught me how to love in a way I could not have imagined from the time you were young. Your ability to set a goal for yourself and see the journey through to accomplishment is more than a parent could ask for. Life has had its ups and downs but still I see you rise. You have taught me that it is ok to speak with a gentle demeanor.

Micha'l: You are your daddy's child. I love your competitive nature and your genuine honesty. If I ever want the harsh truth I need to look no further. We have been through a lot together and I appreciate your willingness to speak your mind and express how you truly feel. You have taught me patience, and how to be a better communicator. Above all, though, you've taught me how other people view me.

Isaiah: You are my quiet storm. You lay back and listen as if you're not paying attention. And at the precise moment you drop a jewel that causes us all to stop and ponder. I know it may seem as though I am harder on you, but that is only because I love you deeply. Your quiet demeanor has touched me and taught me to view life through a different lens.

To my siblings, Darshell and Dawn: Growing up, we were truly "hear no evil, see no evil, and speak no evil". Through thick and thin, more times than not, we had each other's backs. Our journey was not an easy one and we have seen more than our fair share of dysfunction, but we all persevered through, holding each other's hands as needed along the way. You were planted in the concrete but have both grown into beautiful flowers. And, I love you both for that. We inspire each other, lean on each other, and support each other. The way only we can.

Grandma: I wish you could see us now, far beyond what you remember. You taught us all how to fight, how to retreat but to never surrender. You instilled in us the golden rule and admonished us when needed, and it hurts to know the fruits of your labor have now been harvested and you're not here to see it.

Preface

I began my journey as a writer at a young age to mentally escape the reality of being born into a domestic violence-filled, poverty-stricken, and physically abusive existence that was my life. Most of my memories as a child left me feeling lonely and unable to measure up. My grandmother adored my mother's first born. My mother cherished her youngest, and I was left feeling like the abused, bed-wetting, too afro-centric, 'look just like your daddy', middle child cherished by none.

But in my writing, I was the knight in shining armor, the football MVP, and the Oscar-winning performer. I was the love and adornment of all the characters I ever created. My child pen never strayed far from the pad because to me, it was all I had. During college, I began my journey towards higher education. I majored in Psychology and minored in Black Studies. This was the moment my writing evolved from being pity driven to shedding a spotlight on social and cultural disparities, inequities, and deprivations that impact millions of voiceless black and brown people.

I realized that I, in all my African heritage, was enough. I guess you can say that was the moment I got my literary and social swag. My writings are never anti-anyone. They are just always pro-black, whether it is black realization, black love, black wealth, or black injustices. Growing up in the inner city of Cleveland, Ohio on 93rd & Hough (otherwise affectionately known as Hough Heights) never gave me an objective view on other nationalities. But it did introduce me to poverty I could feel, street violence that was real, and a system of disparity that I couldn't imagine someone creating for themselves. So, who created it and why?

My poems speak to this system; they seek to answer the "why" and to redeem the conscience and subconscious mind of those that find themselves in this system. It is my goal that through my poems they will be awakened from their dormancy and once again realize that they are enough.

I have been fortunate enough to have four unique and gifted children who are also a source of my inspiration. Realizing each was conceived in love illuminates the emotional roller coaster ride that love is. Its ups and downs can read like a story of regret or redemption, but the intersection of a relationship is a ripe harvest for poets.

My poetry will incite, entreat, and beseech with the fundamental objective of reaching the reader. I want to provoke thought, and dialogue, about the factors that divide us. I want to empower, embolden, and inform you of what exists in someone else's reality. But even greater still, I want to treat the wound that life has caused to prepare us all to heal!

"Art has to be a kind of confession. I don't mean a true confession in the sense of that dreary magazine. The effort, it seems to me is: if you can examine and face your life, you can discover the terms with which you are connected to other lives, and they can discover, too, the terms with which they are connected to other people...

Most of us, no matter what we say, are walking in the dark, whistling in the dark. Nobody knows what is going to happen to him from one moment to the next, or how one will bear it. This is irreducible. And it's true for everybody. Now, it is true that the nature of society is to create, among its citizens, an illusion of safety; but it is also absolutely true that the safety is always necessarily an illusion. Artists are here to disturb the peace." – James Baldwin

PARDON ME

Pardon me, White Supremacy, for stepping on your shoes

You are under the impression that the first shall be last but the first has never been

You

Would You have preferred Me to just ignore this misunderstanding, when addressing it is long overdue?

The deception began in a distant land with the theft of Ausar, Auset and Heru

The decimations of Alexandria, worship of Serapes set in motion Ptolemy's world view

Our service to the Christ has shackled us twice

We are physically and mentally subdued

Pardon me, White Supremacy, for espousing to embrace a different truth

I would never seek to marginalize Your existence because that would equate to Me being superior to You

*There is no such thing as integration in this country.
Our society is still separate and unequal.*

SEX SELLS

Lust

lasciviousness and sexual perversion

Porn

the strip club beckons with lustful coercion

Rage

injected to steal the innocence of a virgin

Satan

looking for a sacrificial lamb

Fear

of your young being taken is unnerving

Enticement

of the grinding, the winding and twerking

Sinful

desires in our hearts, the inability of curbing

There are two masters to serve, which one are you serving?

The marital bed is undefiled, but is it the only bed deserving?

One good girl is worth a thousand bad Bitches.

THE HUSTLE

You can't out hustle a hustler

Hell! I created that line

Tested it on the masses and it worked every time

Ever out-hustled a phone booth with a drill and some twine?

Dime in

Made the call and with a tug the dime still mine

Now you might out-hustle an old hustler

That's a little feeble of mind

But that Three Card Monte can be hard to follow when the blind is leading the blind

It is said that love is a hustle and to that truth I'm inclined

Because for many years through my blood, sweat, and tears

I was hustled out of my time

Don't Get Hustled

I know it is said that experience is the best teacher, but I pray for the wisdom to learn from others' experiences so that I minimize some of life's wounds. For wise is the man who can avoid the traps that have so ensnared others.

STILL HUNTING

Lustful desires succumb to temptation

Secret rendezvous give way to erotic stimulation

Passions overflow within soulful penetration

You have what you need at home, but you hunt for flirtatious communications

Mysterious encounters fuel these sensations

Look for a way into the streets through deceptive calculation

So that you can overtake your prey that you have vehemently been chasing

At home, your true love: believing, trusting, waiting

Your actions are reckless, contemptible, brazen

You are loyal, except for selfish gratification

We are created to be Gods - is this your interpretation?

As we go, so does our seed, and the advancement of our nation

Are you still chasing a fool's gold? You know when it's time to let go, even if you don't know how. You will wake up one morning and realize the life you were living wasn't really living at all.

RACISM

Racism is the head of a doubled sided coin:

heads you lose, tails you lose

Many have endured this truth since the day they were born

yet we're still confused

We understand its tenets and systemic reach but

many tentacles are hidden from view

We must unite to develop black trust this is

something we have neglected to do

A Pan-African approach to supremacists' tree and rope,

many are stronger than the few

With every chapter turned another lesson learned with

our maturation clearly in view

If we struggle alone in silence, it is only because we are ashamed to struggle openly together. The façade of being "well" is preventing our realization of healing. We Are Stronger Together.

GREATNESS

Greatness is never fully realized; it's just an elaborate idea

It's formed through the unyielding determinations, intent on making the vision clear

When we suffer through the growing pains, we learn to overcome our fears

The desire to endure the highs and lows through the boos and the cheers

Not to sell but to build, foregoing the get rich quick for wealth over the years

For us, by us, employing us, because it is us that we should hold dear

Then and only then will the change we seek appear

No longer slaves to the propaganda

But learning to amass wealth just as our peers

Because our greatness will never fully be realized

Until we learn to draw each other near

Success may not be experienced without struggle. Pleasure may not be realized without pain. But the difficult times in life make our triumph that much sweeter.

RELIGIOUS

"In the beginning" was the beginning according to King James's infallible words

An interpretation of creation that archaeological interpretation could only infer

So eloquently depicted as the first day depicts the establishment of dusk as it gives way to dawn

But who inspired the scrolls? It was God we are told; but God Himself never wrote of what he had done

Could it be the fragmented intellect imagined of men whose fragmentation ushered in the idea of virtue or sin?

Who by their own hands history was penned as the scrolls were historically aligned from beginning to end

Do we accept without question or question its inception?

Is it truly the inerrant word of God or is She open for suggestion?

At what point does fact meet fable? Is it at the same point where truth meets lie?

By religion we live and because of religion we die

When people do not want to deal with the truth of history, I guess they just rewrite it.

STILL RISING

There is a concerted effort to silence the black voice

Make us believe what we saw wasn't what we really saw because reality for them is a matter of choice

The intent is to eradicate our existence and blot out our race

But without us, there is no them, so them want to make sure us niggas stay in our place

Still mentally entangled in the deceptive web they wove

Struggling to realize our own greatness as we unravel our true history of old

Shackles were not our beginning and the master's whip will not be our end

We have walked through the valleys of the shadows of death and we shall rise once again

When push comes to shove, you just make sure you shove that push back! Success is our only option; failure is not.

100 MILES

They say the black man is 100 miles and running and if that's true I'll be

taking aim and gunning

We're past 40 acres and a mule as adequate compensation now we

got more coming

The revolution may not be televised but it's been 400 episodes and the

series is still running

Trying to outwit the fox who maneuvers well in this jungle and is cunning

However, the service has been rendered, the debt accrued, and

the diaspora is dunning

We will not be deterred from your silence or your shunning

Nirvana has exposed us to the true essence of

sunning

It is not always easy to be optimistic. Believing in yourself can be difficult when you feel like you are inferior. But when you truly realize who you are and whose you are, optimism and belief will pursue you.

I APOLOGIZE

I apologize for the adultery that ultimately destroyed what God had made

I was caught up in the selfishness of being me through the orchestration of the

games that I played

I allowed death to enter my spirit while lust commandeered my gaze

I should have been a better man but, instead your love

I betrayed

Yesterday is far beyond my grasp but the lessons learned hover like

death itself

I see more clear the hurt and fear I inflicted with every unfaithful

blow I dealt

I debased the covenant that I committed to extol, fragmented the heart

that was mine to make whole

Apologies abound but will never erase the pain of unfaithfulness toll

I Apologize

Sometimes life gives you a second chance at forever. Learn from your mistakes and embrace the opportunity.

FOREVER MORE

Far from a Herculean matador

Self-assured in search of nothing more

Beyond mere physical conquests

That conflict with my emotional core

I turn to my deeper sense of self

To prepare for what love has in store

No longer restricted by mental boundaries

I'm prepared to travel from shore to shore

In search of the divine

That one of a kind

That I will lovingly address as forever more

I've experienced the shallow encounters

Which produced heartache and disdain

Pouring out my soul into all I knew

And in return nothing but pain

Now I long for something pure of heart

And Forever must be her name

Sometimes life feels like magic. That progressive intoxicating power of positive black love. It is an oxymoron only to those who have never experienced it.

QUALITY

I just want to speak my mind and express what's in my heart

Words of wisdom, doom, and gloom or wherever I choose to start

I love the rising of the sun as well as a tranquil sunset

I can endure the worst of who I am while still espousing my best

I am mindful when I'm riding high and resourceful when times are low

I have learned to stop to protect my heart, but I'm not afraid to grow

I know I can do all things in Him, but I'm not opposed to asking for help

I can stand as one in a million-man march

And if need be

I can stand by myself

I've come to learn that being strong can make the weak feel uneasy. Being unafraid of what tomorrow may hold can frighten others. Your resiliency can cause others to refuse to try. While your intense pursuit of excellence can be a threat to the status quo.

TAKE A KNEE

In School Daze "Wake Up" was the last word exclaimed by Dap

This expression personified by the kneeling of Kap

The idea of disrespecting the flag is just a distortion of facts that ignores the mandate Blue has for black

At what point will our humanity rise and respond to the attacks?

Will justice be awakened or remain sopor like Dak?

We are a nation built on democracy and civil protest is synonymous with that,

But beneath the prevarication the truth is difficult to extract

The foundation of racism has yielded a few cracks but far more nefarious are the laws it enacts

A lawless provocation rooted in a cowardice act where your only crime is your color, now where is the justice in that?

Some people misconstrue confidence for conceit. They confuse your aptitude with the attempt to be arrogant. Your desire for excellence is twisted into a desire for the limelight. But never dumb down who you are to make someone else feel comfortable with who they're not.

A FATHER'S LOVE

I've never carried you in my womb because I don't have that to give

But to love, protect, and nurture your essence is the reason why I live

The illumination of your path to life's pitfalls and snares

The assurance that in your darkest hour, you'll know someone is there

I'm far from being perfect, no matter how hard I try

But I'll forgive thine shortcomings and I can only pray you forgive mine

Teach me how to value seeing things from your point of view

Because my life would be meaningless without the father's love I have for you

This is what I live and will die for.

BASTARD CHILD

If I only had a few things to say, I would say that shit and be done

But God has given me the pen of a ready writer and the fire of an unquenchable tongue

Give ear all ye nations and lend an ear you rulers of earth

For God has given birth to a bastard child and soon shall come the rebirth

Cast away all your folly, for the time of theatrics has since passed

It is time to labor in the garden of self for the days are fading fast

Your mortality will become immortal and your name scribed in blood

For the peace that lies in the depths of your soul will bear witness of His true love

Instead of wasting your existence imitating life, learn how to live and thrive. You already have the seed within you so allow life to provide the rain and the sun.

REVELATION NOT FOUND

We must drown out the static from that which life brings

to realize why the caged bird sings

Allowing us to grasp the impossible is possible if we only accept

the treasure life will soon bring

Feeling the presence of the universe through calming the conscious and

connecting with our subconscious mind

Our frequency tuned past the mundane and channeled to intertwine

with the divine

I am too great to be small minded. My thoughts are so far outside the box that I refuse to be marginalized. My vision sees far beyond tunnel vision and I refuse to pretend that I am blind.

STILL BLAZING

we may be inclined to pass the pussy the same way we've passed the Dutch

eyes glassed over masking the euphoric meditation from the indulgence of too much

from no seeds. no stem. no sticks to more pussy. more ass. more dick

it's that social disconnect that serves to disconnect the belief of being well

when you are sick

being in love with a stripper, making it rain to tip her, for referring to a Queen as a Bitch

I'm not against the need to blaze coupled with the desire to get paid

just not at my peoples' expense

Never succumb to the pressure of just fitting in. Never exchange your individuality for mediocrity. Sometimes in order to find yourself, you must first change who you thought yourself to be.

MA'AT CREED

Hold fast to the promise, give ear to our Ma'at Creed

Neglect not your offspring, enlighten the subconscious seed

Tedious is the road we must travel, and our minds have yet to be freed

But when our darkest hour appears bleak, our hearts still believe

Give ear all my diaspora, the tide will soon recede

All nations will once again bow to thrones at the Mother Land's feet

Our garments have been worn and crowns turned to thorns but Neguses we will always be

Even though life does not always turn out the way we intended, the baton must be passed.

BLACK CRIMINALIZATION

They say Black on Black crime is society's ill, but what they neglect to mention

is how many blacks they've killed

Africa, the Middle Passage, Caribbean, Brazil, Haiti, Britain have been their

slaying fields

Even non-violence was met with disdain, civility was the dream, but the result was

a King slain

Florida's Rosewood, Arkansas' Hoop, Tulsa's Greenwood outlines your

end game

Politicians keep statistics on the crime of black plight while the judicial system

monetizes the value of black life

Black on Black crime was designed to deceive the black mind into believing it is more palatable

To be white

The battles we face are not external but rather internal. The harder the fight the more we must look within ourselves for the resolve to walk in victory.

MY SON

I've watched you grow from a young lad to a grown man son, and my only regret is not being there since day one

Running away from my responsibilities, I got honest, passed down from my Dad
I guess God wanted for you something I never had

You have transitioned through life's cycles and persevered through each change, you've held true to your convictions even when it caused you pain

A turning point in your progression took place when you were Airmen trained
You realized our strength is predicated on the weakest link in our chain

I know you're far from perfect, we've all made mistakes along the way
But never allow another's trapping to bind you to the misapprehensions of yesterday

Your journey is far from over and if I can extend a little advice before you admonish my grandkids take a deep breath and ponder options twice

Realize the difference between Mars and Venus, don't attribute it to mere spite
In order to grow in love, you must quiet your mind to hear the heart of your wife

Acknowledge the power of the Divine because from here your future looks bright

Never allow a moment in time to define who you are, but instead use every moment to redefine who you are and what you can accomplish.

BLACKBIRD

Tell me, Blackbird why can't you fly. Are your wings too weak? Or are you too afraid to try?

I know that ignorance is bliss, but there is power in your reply!

Have you been convinced that your best will never measure up? That destiny's dreams should never be touched?

Have the perils that move through the unknown caused a falter in your trust?

Explain to me, Blackbird, why you haven't taken flight? Have you been weighed down by your circumstance? Or broken by your plight?

Yield not to your fears as to a child's veneration of the night

Allow peace to become your blanket, serenity where your head lies. Take hold of the tribulations because soaring is a birthright.

Until you take that leap of faith you will never experience higher heights!

Realizing your potential is not the same as experiencing the success that your potential produces. Never just settle for your potential.

TORN

Too many misunderstandings rooted in different shades of thought

Relational boundaries being overrun with repetitive lessons being taught

Is it genuinely the real article or just pretense in which I'm caught?

So many lines that intersect, make it difficult to connect the dots

As I lament in my anguish a disdain for its existence begins to ascend

Is it toxic masculinity that rules my thoughts? Or my pride I'm attempting to defend?

Or is it the traumatic realization that all good things eventually come to an end?

Life is never just black and white. There are always shades of gray.

MEDITATE ON THIS

The erudition of the closing of my eyes and model still, with thoughts of turning my can't into I will
the quieting of life's distractions in search of my intrinsic peace allowing the universe to flow through me as I commune with my inner Chi
Beta thinking begins to diminish as my Alpha mentation are unleashed
Theta intellection is my aspiration and Delta cerebration will soon be in reach
the unknown becomes transparent life's limitations no longer encumber, unveiled is the limitlessness of our existence and transcendental meditation feeds the hunger
the Matrix can be axiomatic if every Neo would effectuate our voice
the red or blue pill can open the seal and it's invariably still our free choice

Your conscious thoughts are the oars that propel through the sea of life. But your subconscious mind is the rudder that navigates you to your destiny.

THE PURGE

It's time to put away the error of ill intent that has taken over my soul, as I intend to realize there are things in life I will never be able to control.

Past the point of trying to argue in my heart what is wrong or right, like a brotherhood begins with the idea to never end, until you find out that your brother has slept with your ex-wife!

Or the age-old adage, blood is thicker than water. But when you don't believe what their spirits believe the blood relationships are reduced to mere fodder.

Your childhood dream was to be raised by a king. But he sings to make a prince, raising them has never been his thing.

Let me not forsake the emotional heartbreak when forever begins to fall, then to your surprise, you'll realize that your forever lacked a heart at all.

Before the levy has been breached, we must relieve the trappings of inner grief, if we're ever to enjoy the abundant spoils of internal peace.

It is important to learn how to grow past the grips of hurt because the longer you allow it to hold onto you the more it will hold you back. Free yourself from its grip and you have freed your soul.

MY SEED

The pain is beyond comprehension

it runs deep through my core

The distance at times feels unbearable

the heartache I resist to endure

My child, my offspring, my seed

may as well reside on a distant shore

I lay in anguish and despair

every night that they're not here

There was a time when two became one, and then two again

and I watched them all disappear

My infliction is quenched, and torment relents

with a few encounters each year

What gives way to a social belief

that one parent is above and the other is beneath

I must learn to press forward

because there is no place to retreat

Until we meet again, I'll hold your memories

my child, my offspring, my seed

Take a deep breath and enjoy the sweet scent of the roses, or feel the gentle breeze of the wind, before you continue up the mountain to its peak so that you don't become so obsessed with the destination that you fail to enjoy the journey.

RECKONING

Some cats blow smoke like fire but they never pass the Dutch

Underestimating true game until they're faced with the need to be clutch

Fronting like they're untouchable until they finally get touched

Claiming they can handle it all when all can become a little too much

Mother Earth gave you life and you will return to her as dust

But life between start to finish? That shit's up to us

You may not always be able to control what happens to you in life, but you can control how you respond to life. Choose a positive outlook.

ENIGMA

Life is the enigma that we purport to embrace

because solving the riddles of our existence expands our capacity

beyond time and space

Our inability to comprehend life's profundities undermines our ability to keep pace

We prostitute our dreams for acquiring things that upon death we can neither leave nor take

Let not our gifts lay barren wasted because we moved with such haste

Train up a child in the way they should go eventually endeavoring to take

our place

We may never solve all of life's mysteries but together each riddle we can face

My perspective appears pristine but in truth they're just shattered dreams

Because life is still an enigma and I am left wondering what does it all mean?

The challenges in life can make us better or bitter. Life's ups and downs can produce those who overcome or those that are overtaken. We are born to be victorious. Don't allow life to steal your victory.

FORSAKEN

Caught up in the cycle

(just trying to maintain)

Birthed as Kings and Queens

(who changed the reigns)

Persuaded by miseducation

(preoccupied with fame)

Forsaking the motherland

(while blind to the value of our name)

Pan-Africanism must be our pursuit if

(our destiny is ever to change)

The prodigal son realized the error of his ways and returned home.
Job endured his suffering and refused to lose faith.
Ezekiel experienced dry bones becoming alive again.
So, what's your excuse?

MY COUNTRY 'TIS OF THEE

Past the point of redemption, I've been crushed by my decisions, holding true to a false pretense. How easily I was deceived!

In holding these truths to be self-evident, my life has been reduced to irrelevance by a country overzealous to deracinate my exultancy with no hesitance.

I feel trapped in a system that undermines my isms, whose tactics of white lies never equates too many colors on the reverse side of its prism.

Enduring this distortion of the equality of man, oceans of bereavement, voyaged us to a God-forsaken land.

Oppressed by an Aryan nation in its pursuit of a white master plan.

Resistance to achromatic subsistence inferiority is all that is left.

Exhaling becomes a chore due to oppression's restriction of each breath.

Who would've thought "America's Liberty" was a euphemism for death.

Injustices that take place around the world impact the justice we receive where we reside.

INNER PEACE

Peace descend from the heavens and reveal to me your true

essence

Affirm the deity that's domicile that I may elevate my thoughts

above the present

Expose me to the roots of my lineage and my ancestor's mysticism

and universal lessons

Allow me to feed from your omniscience and continue to feel your

Omnipresence

The labyrinth of life can exacerbate my plight leaving my heart

unassured and reticent

But the peace from within comforts like a friend and will never leave

me jettison

The phrase "You're Deep" relegates itself to how you think, but true depth is determined by what you do. I don't want to just "be deep" in thought. I want the depth of my actions to run parallel with the depth of my convictions. So how deep are you?

LITTLE BLACK BOY

Little black boy, God gave you as a gift, but your nature has been misconceived, so the powers that be, feel the need to stop you and frisk.

Little black boy, twelve is past the age to play with boy toys without assuming the risk, because a toy gun meant for fun can equate to the obituaries list

Little black boy, mind your father and mother when they express a social truth. Don't assume you can do what your white counterparts do because you're looked at differently as a youth.

Savage, animal, subhuman, thief, super predator, miscreant, ignorant, beast: these are the images of you by many whites and the police.

So little black boy! Resist these trends even if the propaganda never ends. We have the fulfillment of a prophecy to defend and we need little black boys
to develop into strong black men.

You will never become who you are destined to be if you continue to listen to those who believe that you're not.

THE TRUTH

The truth of our perceived reality is that this reality lacks truth

Deceptions of the past still train our ass to hate ourselves more than

the colonizer's point of view

It was religion's plan to bind our hands and teach us not to despise the

slave master's rebuke

Through whips and chains, the absence of our names under fear of death

we began to follow suit

The fear of broken dreams and the inability to redeem lost time

Made freedom our only pursuit

As repetitive as it may seem we must once again dream dreams that

trace back to our early roots

We are all connected to the past one way or the other. The foundation that yesterday laid supports the building that we build today.

SPOKEN WORD

The power of the spoken word conceals and reveals,
Cuts deep into our psyche causing reality to appear surreal.
Similes, metaphors and symbolisms transform into expressed speech,
the manifestation of contorted emotions when pure expression is what we seek.
Hiding behind the shadows overshadows life's true intent;
words permit us to sojourn on the path that truth augments.
Whether ideologies audibly conveyed or introspections that alter our ways, a kind word uttered can temporarily hold demons at bay.
When lines become blurred and your silent expectations go unheard, you can find your voice in the power of the spoken word.

Forever is not a destination; it is a commitment to always be an intricate part of the process.

DAMNED IF I KNOW

A poet once dropped that dot-dot ditty dot-dot dash

To illustrate street code that was used in the past

It spoke of racial conspiracies, government acts that would leave you aghast

The concrete jungle intercommunicates a vibe they would never be able to grasp

More than words spoken, it was a movement poised to advance

Through disunity we can be controlled but fortify when unified we stand

Capturing the essence of black power, that which civil disobedience could create

Long since those words transpired, black exponents we are prepared to forsake

The denouement of black movements of yesterday rightfully gives room for pause

Once federal dollars are injected, your vision has succumbed to its ownership clause

Give them an inch, they will take a mile, and eventually they will control it all

What makes us weakened in our resolve, great expectations unable to unfold

Why are we disillusioned with individualism?

The collective compounds growth

When will we wake the hell up?

Damned if I know

Avoiding change will only ensure that you are not prepared for it, but it will not stop change from happening. Meet change head on.

ONE DAY AT A TIME

For every word spoken literally or in jest

That was meant to crush your spirit or grind your heart into dust

The agony of defeat imputable to the failing of each test

The compounding of each anticipation magnified and compressed

Through every hard decision left on your pilgrimage to figure out for you

What good is a partner to travel with when the journey feels like one rather than two?

The dimming of your light and the distortion of your view

That which is beyond your choice because some shit you just wouldn't choose

It was like life was being sucked from your body, bitterness began to accrue

I believe there's a rainbow on the horizon, it's just this day I must get through

The fact that you love me is not as important as how you love me. Your idea of loving me to death may emotionally kill me.

RETURN TO SENDER

I've been sold a perfidious bill of goods by vivacious curves, supple breasts and deceptive eyes

My heart has been opened to the possibility of destruction, darkness agonized through sunshine

Thoughts of grandeur, dreams of forever and the macrocosm laid waste at our feet

A depth of love incomprehensible, unbridled passion and serenity that induce the euphoria of complete

When in turn what was bequeathed was a dubious subsistence, immersed in a selfish line to tow

Where the selfless love protracted is subtlety didactic and deprived of water and sunlight to grow

The very thought of tomorrow diminished, the possibilities of forever
too bleak

The lie becomes opaque, the deceived illuminate, and the continence of the deceiver destroys all beliefs

But I refuse to give way to bitterness, and I resist the ideas that love should
yield or surrender

So, I will just repackage deception back in its box and label it "return to sender"

Travel life's journey with those who are headed in a similar direction. You cannot force your direction or drive on someone else, this will only lead to frustration and unnecessary delays. Instead, fix your mind on the destination, and allow other travelers the opportunity to add to the journey towards your purpose.

LEGACY

Legacy in truth is defined not by what you have but instead by that which you
leave behind.

Generational wealth commences with the decision to plant a seed and the willingness to carry on the task of cultivating the land by each generation that proceeds.

Through trial and error, the times that you succeed and fail continue to inspire the build until black excellence prevails.

Unobtainable through purchase and balanced on the eternal square transferred through my lineage and reinforced by my heirs.

Never relinquishing our progress through willful abdication entrenched in suasion and maintained through unification.

Each brick laid in the foundation forged in determination will be a testament to generational wealth's summation.

Rise above the naysayers, transcend the norm, refuse to accept the limits of others when defining the purpose for which you were born. Turn a deaf ear to the doubters by training that small, still voice. Success is never relinquished, and effort is always a choice.

ALWAYS

You are the inspiration for who I am my muse incarnate, the embodiment

of my soul

You are the lifeline out of my sunken place, the calm when chaos has

taken hold

You are the essence of my reverberation, the channel that is always in tune

If we played the life of Love Jones, I would be your Darius and you would

be my Oshun

I've learned to appreciate every moment together because time passed

can never be regained

You are my embrace and exhale, the happy ending to my fairy tale

because of you my life will never be the same

Never underestimate the Power of Prayer, the Power of Purpose, the Power of Determination and the Power of Love. Because these are the Pillars of Success.

SHUT-'EM DOWN

We must take up arms in our advancement by any means necessary

We must shoulder the weight of those before us and those to come without growing weary

For every comrade fallen in battle, one thousand more are willing to take their place

Life is unto death, so we stand in defiance and death is our only embrace

No longer will our young, mercilessly be gunned down in the street

Without an eye for an eye befittingly applied making the cycle complete

Refusing to perpetuate the stereotype our oppressor chooses to inflict

We must take control of our self-image and the narrative we desire to depict

We must be strong in our conviction while refusing to capitulate or give ground

All those who seek to controvert our cause, we must rise up and

Shut 'Em Down

Without war there can be no progress.

ELEVATION

Life will continue to transcend

where there is beginning there will always be an end

The outpouring of a broken heart at some point begins to mend

As much as we look for acceptance outside ourselves

we eventually must look within

Day will turn to night then night to day again,

this is part of our ontogenesis

the continued opportunity that life extends

Learning how not to allow life to break us even when at times we bend

Acquiescing love and perseverance

to guide us as we run towards the ideas we contend

Realizing that to the extent we know

there exists occurrences in the universe

that are beyond our ability to comprehend

Sometimes, what appears to be right on the surface, is wrong for you, and that which seems wrong, puts you right where you need to be. But the challenge is discerning the difference between the two.

BLACK RIVER

You are a river that flows like the sands of time your passions unmatched your beauty sublime

your zenith expands beyond the heavens your treasures are beyond measure to love you completely is what my heart endeavors

diamonds rubies and sapphires all pale in comparison to the sun I am a King among men whose love is unrelenting and cannot be undone

the currents of your devotion crest beyond the banks of the Nile, the authenticity in your embrace one could never revile

oh daughter to the night dawn to the rising sun you are my ever-true love the prodigious web that the universe has spun

with stories yet to be told teachings destined to unfold you are the incarnate of which the gods had foretold

Black River

Never take for granted the beauty that has been cultivated in a relationship. Black Love is intoxicating, don't resist the libation.
Hotep

THIS OLD HOUSE

It is just a matter of time before this old house gives way

The bow has bowed, and the foundation has decayed

What once was strong, now life's winds cause to sway

The roof was once its strength; now it's unable to keep the rain at bay

The yard a vast emerald green, now brown patches, thorns, and thistles restrict play

The place that once was home to so many dreams now refuse to allow any to stay

When it was strong no one saw to its needs, now its force has drifted away

Time will overtake every man no matter your status or pay

I knew it was just a matter of time; this old house sure has seen better days

I never get obsessed with yesterday because I'm too busy using today to build tomorrow's successes.

FIGHT THE POWER

We have been marginalized, ostracized, demonized, and traumatized

but now is not the time to compromise

We need to devise a plot, emerging from the front line and shoot our shot, get to the getting while the getting still can get got

Experiencing that 4:44 as exclaimed by Jigga, never forgetting old man river that through the middle passage was fed with dead nigga

Enthralled at the sight of supremacy at the end of our trigger prepared to fight the power of racism whose generation wealth was amassed through rigger

Taking back what was stolen, matching what is brought, we are tired of being fucked on the bottom we aspire to fuck on top

It is said that the revolution won't be televised but whether it is our not, we'll be in the streets fighting, too busy to watch

Fight The Power

They will never 'give' us justice. So if we are afraid to fight and die for justice, then we will never have justice.

DOWN ASS

Sometimes you need a down ass chic that ain't afraid to grab her crotch and hocks when she spits

You tell her to neck Mr. Johnson she replies right after you kiss Ms. Clit

Politically incorrect but that girl is down as shit, her academic status could be straight street or a four-year degree, she is far from being a thot, real is what she prefers to be

When you encounter this breed, soft niggas may choose to flee

There's a toll to pay when you cross her path because down ass chics are loyal beyond belief

A little rough around the edges sometimes rude and a bit crass but when it's time to put in work she ain't afraid to show that ass

She could be that around the way girl or VP of marketing and sales, a hustler in every sense of the word, making moves while niggas chase tail

This is not intended to belittle my sisters but to acknowledge there's another breed among the ranks

You know the characteristics of a down ass chic even if a down ass chic is what you ain't

The cover is only part of the story. What's between the pages is who we truly are. Resist being window dressing; espouse to be the genuine article.

LILY

She is truly the Lily of the Valley with nectar so sweet,

her petals call after days of dawning my hunger longs to eat.

My mouth is filled with her pleasure as honey yields itself to the bee;

I am enamored by her silhouette as darkness begins to retreat.

When I lay between her secret garden, uninhibited by time or space,

I am overwhelmed by the love that radiates from her presence and I long to stay in this place.

If you have ever encountered this lily, you would forever remember her name,

for she will open your eyes to love and your countenance will be forever changed.

We all are in search of our greater selves; unfortunately sometimes that greatness can only be realized when we connect with the part of us that resides in someone else. Never stop striving to be great.

STAY WOKE

There is a saying: "Black Man Stay Woke" but the miseducation of us and our kids

blurs the reality of what woke is

Keep your eye on the man, he will pillage and rape but instead of protecting we are brainwashed to forgive

Believing we can legislate civility, when in reality, civility is what lies at the core

of a man

Humanity is not the pursuit, it conflicts with the corporate brand

Approaching our existence hunched over, curved spine and backs

never straight

Reserved to request the crumbs from their table instead of demanding an equally

portioned plate

We may confess to be enlightened but shrink back when provoked

Maybe we have misconstrued the act of slumber with the idea of being woke

Stay Woke

We are so slave-minded at times with our "boot licking" thinking, that even when the light is turned on and a lie is exposed, we turn off the light believing that it's better to live in the dark.

WRITER'S WRITE

It is said that my pen will forever be true to the locution that flows within, my greatest consequence immortalized over captivating words but then

To my ascetic darkness that chronicle my passion as I partake of the forbidden fruit, calamity appears indignation sears, and I'm blemished by open rebuke.

It is said the affliction will enjoin the narrative in search of intrinsic truth, peering into my soul when heartless and cold has rendered the lines askew.

Is there a moment in our dispensation for us to cry into the universe that God would see fit to create us anew?

Or is this just our lot whether we like it or not? It is forbidden to petition for a more eloquent view.

With my apprehensions dispelled and my efforts impaled,

I will allow this pen to scribe the story that destiny is destined to tell and after the ink has long since dried, you would have learned to know me as well.

No one in humanity, with the exception of God himself, has ever conquered perfection. With this in mind it is important to show a level of humility and contrition when we judge the behavior of others because our behavior may be closer to theirs than we think.

LYNCHING

That Mississippi justice in the modern-day era is on the rise but with the current climate of our political discourse, should we really be that surprised?

The racially charged rhetoric monkeying up how we decide, unifying is not the artifice because conquering works best when you divide.

Oklahoma's Moreland and Smith, Virginias's Collins, Missouri's Jones may as well have hung as strange fruit from the poplar tree before their spirits had gone on home.

Two hundred and forty attempts to properly criminalize but our oppressor duly abstained, because fear is a useful deterrent when your main objective is to constrain.

Barbarianism of the past is still close within reach, whaling cries and tears from a mother's eyes fall on deaf ears to those she beseech.

If we are deprived of our inalienable rights to witness these better days,

Then we are responsible to the diaspora to ensure the rope swings both ways.

If you believe kindness kills hate, then there must not be enough kind people on the earth or, hate is more resilient than we think.

CAUSE AND EFFECT

There are universal principles designed to keep our life in check such as right, wrong, sowing, reaping, cause and effect.

The energy you transmit should be the energy you expect, decoding the intentions of ambiguity will only set the precedence of regret.

If you sow discourse, deception, and the seeds of disrespect, then that will be your portion when the harvest is time to collect.

Financial irresponsibility may create the ostentation of respect, but the end thereof is material love and the trappings of unsurmountable debt.

Live reckless in these streets through distribution and slick speech and be denied your next breath, for you have reaped the harbinger of death.

Stay true to your sentiment even when others are quick to protest. Work diligently in your garden and the fulfillment of purpose you can expect.

A visionary's realization is predicated on his ability to confect: succeed or fail, lead or trail, is inevitably cause and effect.

The decisions we make have real consequences, not just for ourselves, but they can impact all of those that are depending on us to get what we need so that you can give them what they need. You Grow; We Grow.

HIP-HOP

Much love to the musicians who seek to drop knowledge and set our minds free

The most Def in this Common era that lyrically personifies Kweli

The Quest of a tribe sojourning through the clan of Wu in search of the militia PE

Our essence as exclaimed by the Queen's name its unity of which we should speak

The production of Boogie down gave ear to street sound digitized over Swiss beats

A movement born from a culture savagely torn to express our anguish and grief

To all musicians who sacrificed selfish ambition to improve our cultural beliefs

Hip-Hop to the core no Bugatti and whores when our young are dying in these streets

We are a rhythmic people whose sound speaks to our subconscious and reverberates through the universe as eternal energy. They are cognitive of the power of sound, that's why execs try to dumb it down.

NOTE TO SELF

Have you ever imagined your last day, the last thing you saw, the last feelings felt, the last dreams dreamt, before your last breath?

What did you neglect to accomplish? How much of you went still, unused? Was your existence rich in fervor, or from light's well you seldom drew?

What words personify your embodiment? What accomplishments resonated as your crowning jewel? Have you lived life as unto wisdom or cast your gifts before fools?

Upon the decimation of your mortal temple the final moments of vitality flashing before your eyes, will it be latent personified or the ancestor's esteem for prodigious realized?

I wrote a note to myself chronicling the study of my nethermost permanence in hopes of discovering what's beneath my exoteric shell.

Enlightened through the peregrination of the lessons life has dealt, I will continue to sojourn until my flesh has gone, penning *My Note to Self...*

We are quick to exegete the text of other people's lives while being comfortable with the eisegesis of our own. Learn to be a student of self. This may make you less critical of everyone else.

About the Author

R.A. McAlpine *(affectionately known as Alpine) is a native of Cleveland, Ohio. Over the past 35 years, he has honed his skill in the writing craft. Although his pen expresses itself beyond poetry, the spoken word has always been his first love. His past liberal work has culminated into a collection of poems entitled Ramology: Note to Self. In addition to writing, he is also an accomplished stage actor who has performed in a number of iconic productions at the historic Karamu Performing Arts Theatre including his first lead role as Chad Deity, in The Elaborate Entrance of Chad Deity. Other credits include the classic play the Color Purple (prized fighter Henry Brodnacks (Buster)), cast member of the published original work Mighty Scarabs (Charles "Killer" Davis), and the captivating play God's Trombones (Pharaoh). Receiving his MBA from Ohio University, Alpine is also a trial tradesman, entrepreneur, and an advocate for fathers' rights. Alpine currently resides in Atlanta, Georgia and enjoys spending time with family and friends, golfing, fitness, fine dining, and is an avid motorcyclist.*

These poems are a powerhouse! They are poignant, prolific, and pure. Alpine's voice is a force to be reckoned with, and he doesn't shy away from the uncomfortable social issues and injustices. He apologizes for nothing, and confronts the reader head-on with difficult topics and themes. His use of vocabulary skirts clichés by presenting 'ugly' words in such an honest and straightforward fashion. He has stood up and said: "This is the reality. Read it. Absorb it. Feel it."

Editor, Janelle Shields

"It is vain that we talk of being men, if we do not the work of men. We must become valuable to society in other departments of industry than those servile ones from which we are rapidly being excluded. We must show that we can do as well as they. When we can build as well as live in houses; when we can make as well as wear shoes; when we can produce as well as consume wheat, corn and rye - then we shall become valuable to society. Society is a hard-hearted affair. With it the helpless may expect no higher dignity than that of paupers. The individual must lay society under obligation to him or society will honor him only as a stranger and sojourner."

- Frederick Douglass

Strive for greatness without selling your soul. Expect excellence without crushing the spirit of others. Realize your independent nature while realizing that there is strength in togetherness. Reach for the heavens without forgetting to reach back and help someone else along the way. For this is the essence of COMMUNITY and we are the COMMUNITY!

- R. A. McAlpine